The Face Painter

Rebecca Siddiqui
Photographs by Lindsay Edwards

Contents

Mom's Work	2
Mom's Paint Box	4
Painting Faces	6
After Work	12
Glossary	16

Mom's Work

My mom is a face painter. She has a clown suit and a blue wig for her work.

Mom paints boys' and girls' faces to make them smile.

Mom's Paint Box

Mom has a box of paints for face painting.

Her favorite paints are red, yellow, and green.

She has a lot of **brushes** in the box, too.

Mom needs her **paint box** at work.

Painting Faces

On Saturdays, Mom paints children's faces at parties and at fairs.

Some days,
Mom works at our school.
She paints children's faces
for concerts and plays.

Some boys want to be tigers.
They want to look scary.

Mom puts lots of stripes and black whiskers on the boys' faces.
Now they are scary tigers.

Mom is very good at painting tigers, dinosaurs, pirates, and butterflies.

She likes to paint beautiful fairies best of all.

After Work

After work,

Mom takes off her clown suit.

Then she cleans her face.

She washes the brushes

and lets them dry.

Then she puts them

back in her paint box.

Mom loves her work as a face painter.

Glossary

brushes

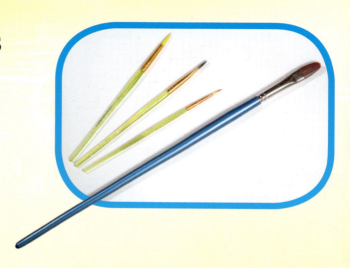

paint box